It was way past bedtime when the detective rapped on the door.

Everyone was still awake, of course, and Mum and Dad were grateful for the company.

'**Good evening,**' the detective said. 'Sorry to bother you so late, but I'm hot on the trail of a master criminal. The most devious supervillain the world has ever seen.'

'The Boogeyman?' asked Mum.

'The Boogeylady?' gasped Dad.

The detective shook her head…

'Somebody much more dangerous. A true agent of chaos.

It's The Cutest Baby in the World.'

'Oh!' said Mum.
'Well, he isn't here.'

'Definitely not,' said Dad.

'Count yourself lucky,' said the detective, 'because if The Cutest Baby in the World gets a hold of you, he will make you do *dastardly* deeds.'

'What kind of deeds?' asked Mum.

'You will speak in a silly voice.

You'll sing made-up songs and dance the chicken dance.

You will find yourself doing anything to make him smile.'

'*Anything?*' asked Dad.

'Anything,' said the detective.

'You will be held captive, like a prisoner.'

'In a dungeon?' asked Dad.

The detective shook her head. 'By his nap time.

He will cover you in yoghurt and dribble and boogers.

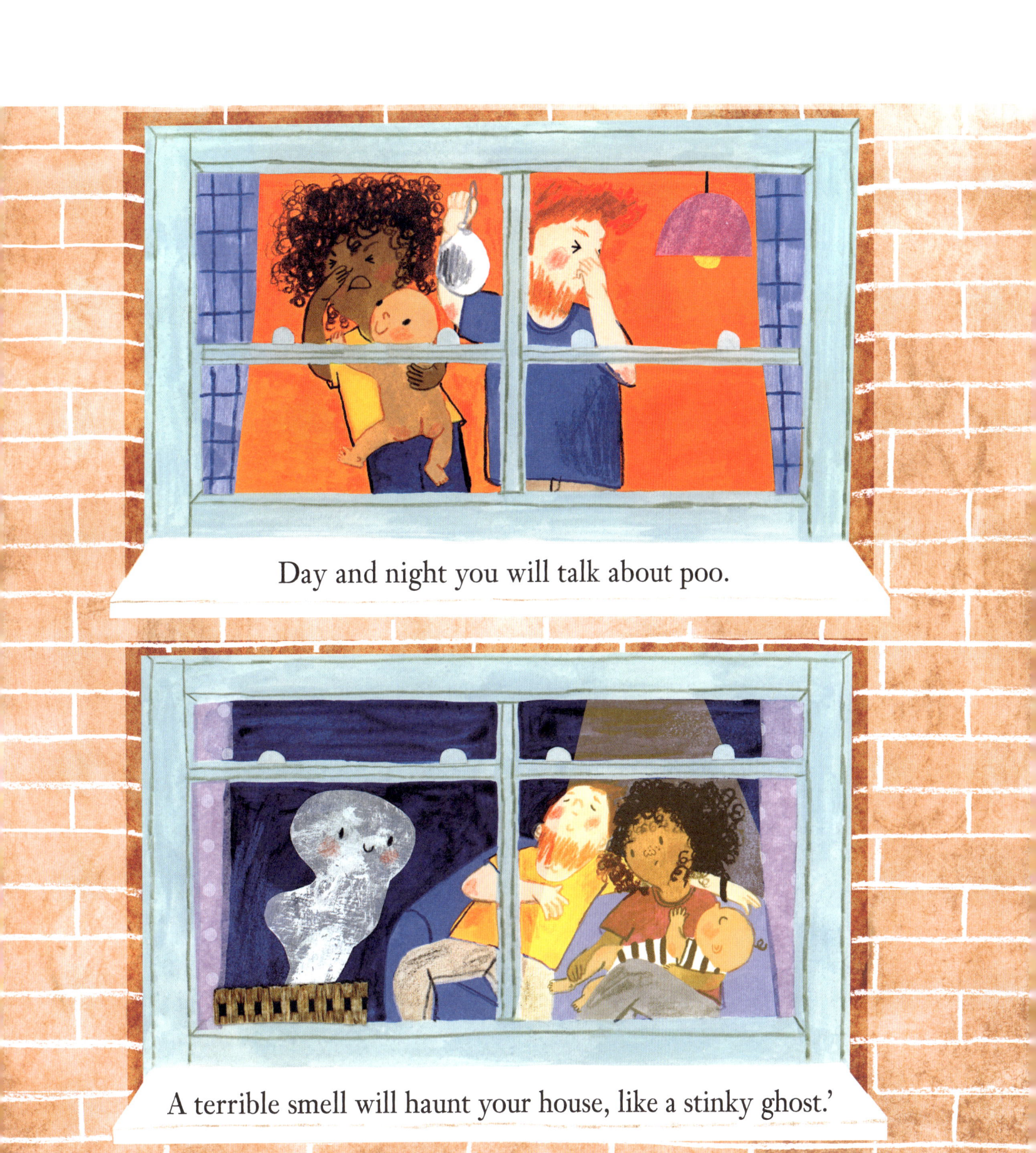

Day and night you will talk about poo.

A terrible smell will haunt your house, like a stinky ghost.'

'You will read the same book over and over until your voice is a tiny squeak. And if he doesn't get his own way...'

'What then?' Mum gasped.

'He
      will
           cry.'

'Eventually, you will lose all your friends.'

'Because of the crying?' asked Dad.

'Or the boogers?' asked Mum.

'The poo smell?' asked Dad.

'Those too,' admitted the detective. 'But mostly because you will show them way too many photos of The Cutest Baby in the World.

He will make you spend all your money on berries...'

'And then he will throw them all up in the air, like wedding confetti.

You will cook him healthy little pancakes
that he will smoosh straight into the carpet.'

'He will empty every drawer. He will pull things out of the cupboards. Your house will fill with junk until there isn't even room for –

Wait a minute,' said the detective, as she looked around suspiciously.

'Are you sure he hasn't been here?'

'Nuh-uh,' said Mum.

'Definitely not,' said Dad.

'Well, beware,' said the detective. 'Stay on guard. He will not hesitate to steal.'

'My jewellery?' asked Mum.

'My video games?' gasped Dad.

'Worse,' the detective whispered…

'Your heart.'

'And just when you think you have escaped his tyrannical reign, you might be tempted to do it all over again.'

'Thank you for the warning, Detective,' said Mum.
'We'll be sure to keep a lookout,' said Dad.

'What people need to know,' the detective said, 'is that once you encounter The Cutest Baby in the World, life will never be the same.'

And wouldn't you know, the detective was right...

Life was never the same again.

To Mum and Dad,
Thank you x
SZ

For tired parents everywhere –
your tiny master criminals are lucky to have you.
And for my own Cutest Baby, a true villain
and an excellent companion.
DB

First published in Australia in 2026 by Thames & Hudson Australia
Wurundjeri Country, 132A Gwynne Street, Cremorne, Victoria 3121

First published in the United Kingdom in 2026 by Thames & Hudson Ltd
6–24 Britannia Street, London WC1X 9JD

WANTED: The Cutest Baby in the World © Thames & Hudson Australia 2026

Text © Davina Bell 2026
Illustrations © Sarah Zweck 2026

29 28 27 26   5 4 3 2 1

The moral rights of the author and illustrator have been asserted.

All rights reserved. No part of this publication may be reproduced or transmitted in
any form or by any means, electronic or mechanical, including photocopy, recording or any other
information storage or retrieval system, without prior permission in writing from the publisher.

ISBN 978-1-760-76532-3

EU Authorized Representative: Interart S.A.R.L.
19 rue Charles Auray, 93500 Pantin, Paris, France
productsafety@thameshudson.co.uk
www.interart.fr

 A catalogue record for this book is available from the National Library of Australia

A CIP catalogue record for this book is available from the British Library

Front cover: illustration by Sarah Zweck, design by Stephanie Spartels
Design: Stephanie Spartels
Printed and bound in China by C&C Offset Printing Co., Ltd

Thames & Hudson Australia wishes to acknowledge that Aboriginal and Torres Strait Islander peoples
are the first storytellers of this nation and the Traditional Custodians of the land on which we live and work.
We acknowledge their continuing culture and pay respect to Elders past and present.

thamesandhudson.com.au

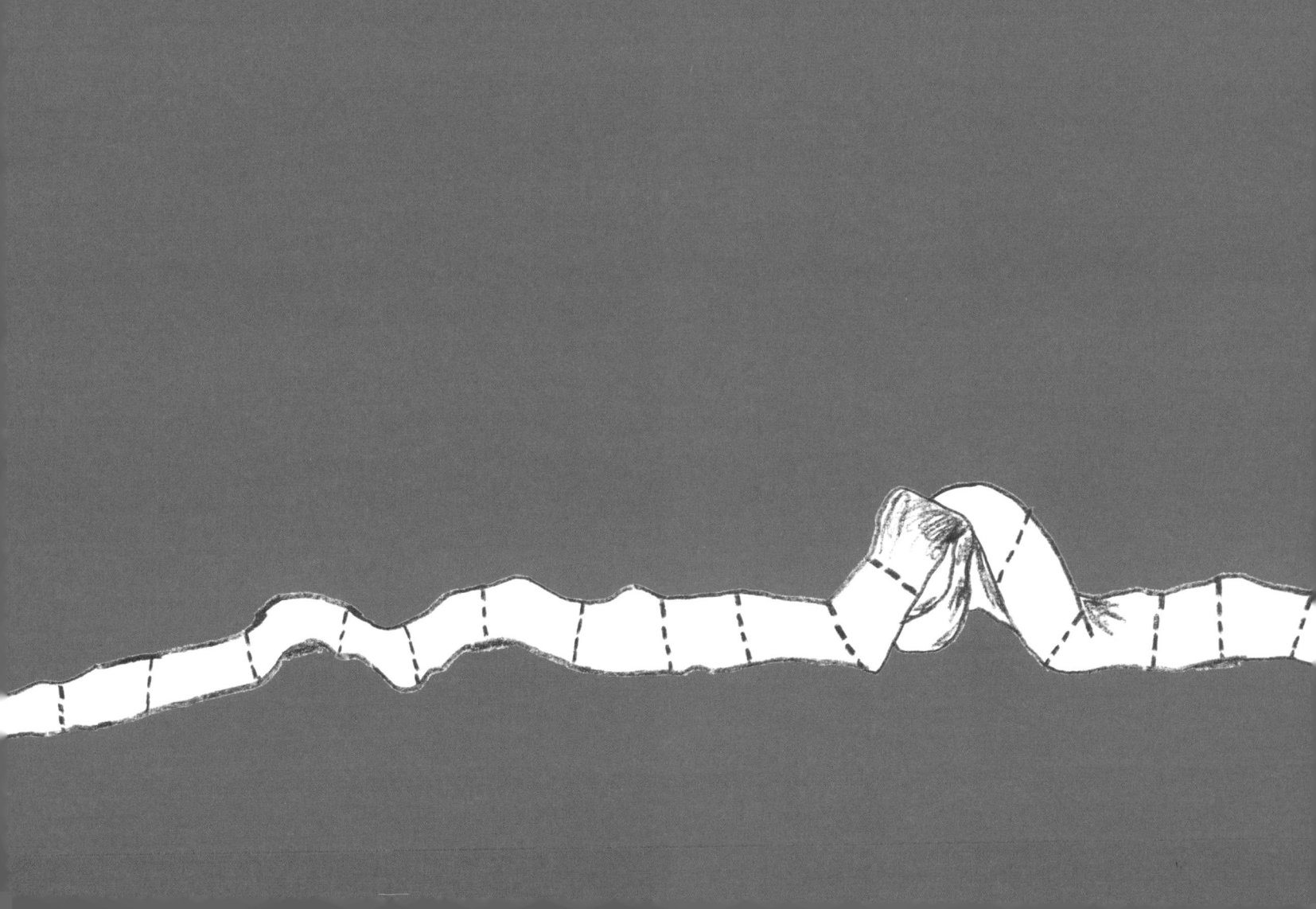